PREPARING FOR INDEPENDENT

AND OTHER PRIVATE SCHOOLS

PREPARING FOR INDEPENDENT

AND OTHER PRIVATE SCHOOLS

A HANDBOOK FOR PARENTS AND GUARDIANS OF STUDENTS PREPARING FOR INDEPENDENT SCHOOLS, PAROCHIAL SCHOOLS, AND OTHER PRIVATE SCHOOLS

Winnie Eke, PhD

ANOINTED LIFE PUBLISHING COMPANY

Phoenix, Arizona

PREPARING FOR INDEPENDENT AND OTHER PRIVATE SCHOOLS

A HANDBOOK FOR PARENTS AND GUARDIANS OF STUDENTS PREPARING FOR INDEPENDENT SCHOOLS, PAROCHIAL SCHOOLS, AND OTHER PRIVATE SCHOOLS

© Copyright 2015 Winnie Eke.
All rights reserved. No portion of this book may be reproduced, stored in a retrieval system or transmitted in any form electronic, mechanical, photocopy, recording or any other except for brief quotations in printed reviews, without prior consent of the publisher.

Printed in the United States of America
Library of Congress Cataloging-In-Publication Data
Eke, Winnie
Preparing for Independent and Other Private Schools / Winnie Eke
Library of Congress Control Number: 1-2319199531

ISBN: 978-0-9906465-6-3   Softcover

Editing and book design by Keith H. Chambers
Cover Design by C W Technology Consulting

www.anointedlifepublishing.com

Dedication

This book is dedicated to the following:

- My family and friends.
- My children for prompting me to do something to help more parents and their children, and for reviewing the original manuscript.
- My friends who have sought my help throughout the years.
- My mom and dad for teaching me the joy of participating in my community.

"It is wretched taste to be gratified with mediocrity when excellent lies before us"

-------Isaac Disraeli

Contents

Dedication v

Preface.. ix

Acknowledgements xi

Introduction xiii

Chapter 1 **Overview of Independent and Parochial Schools** .. 1

Chapter 2 **The Decision Making Process**................................9

Chapter 3 **A Strategy for Choosing the Right Type of School** 13

Chapter 4 **Visit the Schools under Consideration** 21

Chapter 5 **Financial Aid** 25

Chapter 6 **Final Visits and Interviews** 29

Chapter 7 **Admission Tests**..33

Chapter 8 **Acceptance**... 37

Chapter 9 **Other Considerations**.. 39

Preface

In urban cities, many parents and/or guardians enroll their children in local public schools. And, in an ideal world, public school is the best option for parents who would like to use the savings for higher education. However, as their children move up to transition grades five, six, and eight, some wish there were an alternative; for different reasons. But too often, it is these same parents, especially minority parents, who believe they have no option but to accept the schools that their children are assigned to.

Understanding that choices are available is an important first step. Nevertheless, the next step: actually preparing children to make a transition to a new school is not easy for the child or the parents. The undertaking is even more daunting when it is compounded by a multitude of tasks with no simplified roadmap for parents to follow.

This handbook is designed to help parents through the process of preparing themselves and their children for the challenges that lie ahead. It may not answer all questions, but it will highlight most of the common ones and those that I deem essential. It was inspired as a result of what I, as a parent, went through in the transition to an alternate educational experience with my own children.

Acknowledgements

I am indebted to the Director of Admissions at Fontbonne Academy and the Office of Admissions at the Dana Hall School.

I extend my sincere gratitude to Dr. Stan Howard for uplifting me with his work.

I give thanks to Carolyn and Keith Chambers for guiding me through the publishing process.

Introduction

Today, there are different kinds of schools as states and the federal governments have responded to the challenges of educating all children. Included in these innovations are pilot schools and Horace-Mann charters that are under the city system. There are also state charter schools, and private or contracting charter schools— *independent contractors chosen to manage schools that are considered sub-standard because of their state standardized scores.*

Curiously however, in the midst of these innovations, parents who wish to improve their child's education are more confused than ever. It can be a challenge for someone, who may be already stressed to their limits, to have to carve out time to read the pros and cons of each school type and match it against the interests of their child. It does not help that these new innovative schools are not very transparent—they often <u>do not</u> provide enough information for an intelligent decision.

It is almost like a maze; so parents need a resource to digest all the possibilities of the type of educational system that they desire for their children. This book is a guide for those who want to research and make an informed decision on enrolling in an independent (private school) or parochial school.

Chapter 1

Overview of Independent and Parochial Schools

Before going further into any discussions, it is best to define and discuss the different schools and the characteristics of each one. First, there are independent schools; what we generally refer to as private schools. Then, there are schools that are a part of religious institutions and their doctrine. These parochial schools include: Catholic, Christian, Jewish, Russian, Islamic, and Arabic, etc. For this handbook, only independent and Catholic schools will be discussed. Parents and students seeking information on other specialty schools should contact those schools directly.

To enroll a prospective student in an independent or parochial school, a parent must be both positive and proactive. They must be willing to ask many questions and then be prepared to act. It is also important, in the process, to understand the role of these schools in society and why they are needed.

Background Information

In considering enrolling a child in an independent or Catholic school, there is certain information that is important for parents to know. For instance, having a good knowledge and understanding of the organization that operates a particular school, as well as its history, is very important. Nevertheless, I like to caution parents that organizations always put forth a positive spin to attract enrollees. As a result, most of the information that is provided should be viewed as a starting point and only serve as a basis to guide parents in making further investigation. Both independent and Catholic schools have background information that is readily available to the public for review.

Catholic Schools

The National Catholic Education Association (NCEA) provides background information that can be accessed via the web—there is a variety of information on Catholic schools. Included is data on the number of Catholic schools in the country, the parish tuition for both elementary and secondary levels, as well as teacher to student ratios.

For the latest academic year (2012-2013) reported, the association stated that there were approximately 1.9 million students enrolled in Catholic education, at all levels. The report further explained that those students were enrolled in 6,594 Catholic elementary and secondary schools throughout the United States. The breakdown of the 1.9 million enrollments showed that 1,395,793 students were at the middle school level (6th, 7th, and 8th grades) whereas 582,785 students were at the secondary school level (grades 9-12). The NCEA also operates single-gender schools (boys only or girls only). There were 73 single-gender elementary schools and 374 single-gender secondary schools.

The schools, according to the report, were located throughout the country with the largest enrollments in urban areas that included: New York, Chicago, Boston, San Francisco, Miami, Washington D.C., St. Louis, and Cleveland. More than 50% of the largest enrollments were in urban and inner-city areas. The association's report also documented a 99% graduation rate and a 97% college enrollment.

Although these statistics can seem overwhelming, they give parents an idea about the number of schools and how they are in line with the goals that they have for their children. I suggest that parents and their prospective students keep an open mind as they read about and visit the schools of their choice.

It is important for those looking to enroll their child into a particular parochial school, especially a Roman Catholic one, to inquire about the financial standing of the school and its ability to remain open and functional. This could be an issue if the child is expected to graduate from the chosen school.

Another important aspect is the tuition involved in these schools, as well as any additional fees. The NCEA documented that the average tuition is about $3,880 per student for elementary and middle schools, whereas $9,622 is the average for high schools—with fees and other costs, the actual amount is closer to $11,790. It is also important to point out that there is no formal central scholarship or funding for Catholic schools. Nevertheless, financial aid is available. Individuals can apply for financial aid through the Archdiocese school offices.

It should also be noted that the underlying focus for most parents, who choose a Catholic school, is their belief in Christian values; that they equate with moral virtue, high academic standards, and a safe environment.

On this, the NCEA concurs, citing their educational experience as "value-added" and conducted in a safe environment.

Independent Schools

Independent Schools are under the umbrella of the National Association of Independent Schools (NAIS). As is the case with Catholic schools, independent schools under the NAIS, state that parents choose their schools because of the quality of education that they provide. These qualities include: individual attention, small class sizes, teacher excellence, high academic standards, and a safe environment. The NAIS states that they have a long-standing record of academic success; citing US Department of Education studies that confirm their claim.

NAIS membership also includes pre-college nonprofit and accredited schools by NAIS approved accreditation organizations and schools that have been in operation for at least five years. According to recent information regarding NAIS, for the 2010-2011 school year, there were 1,400 schools in the United States serving more than 562,000 students; supported by 121,000 teachers, administrators, and other staff.

It is important to note that tuition and fees are expensive in independent schools. There are no fixed amounts as there are a lot of variables involved such as location (area of the country) and the available resources in each school. Regardless, it is always important to work with each school, because admission is not always determined by the ability to pay. On the other hand, admission does not guarantee free tuition or financial aid.

The NAIS operates a subsidiary called School and Students Services (SSS). This subsidiary collects all completed parent financial statements (PFS) and uses the same criteria for all applicants. Consequently, there is consistency regarding recommended financial awards for each child. However, individual schools make the final decision; depending on how much they have available for financial aid. Parents should make sure all forms and supporting materials are submitted on time.

Regarding academics, studies have shown that NAIS students are enrolled in advanced courses more than public, parochial, and other private schools. Studies have also indicated that independent school students do more homework, watch less television, are more likely to participate in sports, and are better disciplined. To be clear, the issues of doing homework and watching less television depend on parents and the home environment. Establishing rules for homework and providing a quiet place for studying are some of the parental tactics advocated by both types of schools.

Students who board (live on campus) have to abide by each school's rules and regulations. Again, regardless of the circumstances, parents have the ultimate control on the type of behaviors that they need to enhance to enable their children be successful in school. Having enforceable rules appear to be best for all students.

When it comes to sports, there may be differences between independent and either Catholic or public schools. For example, the idea of participating in sports should be encouraged in all schools, but these activities may be curtailed in public schools because of the number of students enrolled and a lack of funding. On the other hand, in Catholic schools there may be fees involved that could limit the ability of some students to participate.

Variations in Independent Schools

There are different kinds of independent schools. Some are day schools only; although others have boarding capabilities (mostly starting at grade nine). There are co-educational schools as well as single-gender schools. Some independent schools are a century old, whereas some are new or relatively new. The structure of each school may be different in terms of how the school is operated and its focus.

Independent schools serve a variety of students. Some offer specialized programs that range from fine and performing arts, to photography classes. Some excel in experiential (the process of learning through experience) learning projects and travel abroad programs. Still others specialize in teaching gifted students and those with learning disabilities. Because of these potentially different focuses, it is important for parents to carefully examine the schools and programs that will be the best fit for their child.

There are many and varied reasons why parents want their children to attend an independent or parochial school. Some consider it a family tradition, but many others choose private or parochial schools because of what they perceive as a failure of the public schools to promote their personal religious values, to provide a quality education, and to ensure a safe environment. Whatever the motivation for choosing an independent or parochial school, extensive planning must be made in advance.

Chapter 2

The Decision Making Process

Many parents start thinking about enrolling their children in a parochial or independent school when their public school children are in transition grades five (5) and eight (8). Some start thinking of alternative schools when they notice that their child is not being challenged or when there are problems in the current school. Other parents prepare their children, as a family tradition, as early as kindergarten or first grade. I have met parents who have made multiple decisions regarding alternative schools—they have had their children in both a public and a parochial school before finally settling on an independent school.

It is interesting to note that some parents made a conscientious decision not to enroll their children in an independent or Catholic school at an early age. Instead, they chose for their child to remain in a public school during their early years to better allow them to understand the intricacies of urban social living.

Decisions Should Be Goal-Driven

Many parents stated that their goal for sending their children to an independent or Catholic school was to make sure that they continued with the type of discipline that had been established at home—where there were routines in place for homework, projects, and extra curricula activities. In essence, they were looking for schools to reinforce those positive behaviors and maintain the discipline that the child was accustomed to. It is therefore important that parents choose schools that will emphasize the same goals that they have, and more, for their children.

It does not necessarily matter why a parent decides to transition their child from a public school to a Catholic or independent school, or even start their child's education in an alternative school; what matters most is that parents know what they want and expect from the school that they choose. The focus should always be on how the school will support their child's education based on his/her needs.

Include Older Children in the Decision

One of the most important aspects of the decision making process is who participates. This is essential for parents with students who will transition from middle school to high school. For children of that age, it is always advisable to include them in the decision-making and choice of schools. Older children like to be involved in decisions that affect them, and that makes the preparation and transition easier for the family. If, on the other hand, they perceive that they are being forced to make the transition, they tend to resist.

My own experience in <u>not</u> including one of my daughters in the decision was a big lesson for me. In the first year, she resisted all attempts by the teachers to help her. Fortunately, she eventually made new friends and became more comfortable in the school; learning how to navigate through all of its protocols.

Having learned from my mistake, I made sure that I included my other children in the decision and let them make the final choice to either stay in a public school or to change to an independent or Catholic school. To aid in the process, I put two criteria in place.

First, I discussed the reasons for the potential transfer with each child. For those that opted to continue in public school, I looked for ways to be in constant communication with the teachers to monitor any lapses on the part of my children.

Secondly, if they chose an independent or Catholic school, they were allowed to pick the particular school that they liked and explain the reasons for their choice. After a while it became easier, as those children advised their younger sibling on the advantages and/or disadvantages of the same.

Make the Decision for Younger Children

For younger children, parents should be decisive—make the choice and let the child know as early as possible. Be sure to ask the child about her/his interests. An effort should be made to explain the entire process so that the child will understand what is involved. This is important, just in case he or she is not accepted into the school. The fact is, there are a relatively few schools available compared to the number of students seeking admission to them.

Chapter 3

A Strategy for Choosing the Right Type of School

As I stated earlier, there are a relatively few number of independent or parochial schools available to choose from, compared to the number of students who would like to attend. For this reason, as soon as parents have decided to choose an alternative school, they should start the process by mapping out a strategy; as soon as possible.

Choosing an Independent School

If one is interested in an independent school, the web is a good place to start. Parents can consult "The Independent School Digest" to find a list of prospective schools that they might like their child to attend. I encourage parents to read the excerpts that are provided, including the mission and vision of each school.

Parents looking into independent schools should consider boarding versus day school for secondary students, as well as single-gender or coeducational.

They should also research each school's area of specialization. For instance, some schools focus on experiential learning projects and some even have study abroad programs. Still others have strong curriculums in the fine and performing arts; or specialization in teaching gifted children and those with learning disabilities. Individual schools can be contacted to obtain their brochures and application materials; however, a visit to the school's website may suffice.

Although many independent schools want academically exceptional candidates, some are working hard to integrate their schools and therefore welcome all students. What those schools look for, in lieu of a high grade point average, is commitment to learning, good social behavior, and one who takes personal responsibility. Nevertheless, to some extent, a good academic history, as well as student involvement and interests in other school activities are needed when a school has to make difficult choices from a large applicant pool, for the slots available are few.

During my canvassing of schools for my children, I found that talking to other parents, who already had children enrolled, was very crucial in helping me to start the process and to ultimately make a good decision. My goal of encouraging the development of leadership abilities in my children enabled me to make decisions about single-gender versus co-ed schools, and boarding versus day schools. And, on one particular web visit to an independent school, I saw the published works of alumni that made a good and big impression on me.

Traditional versus Progressive Independent Schools

For independent schools, parents should consider if the schools that they are looking into are traditional or progressive. Traditional schools have a formal schedule and concentrate mainly on academics. They follow a format similar to that of a public school.

On the other hand, progressive schools have a schedule and a curriculum that adheres to the needs of the student body. Many progressive schools belong to what is known as the Coalition of Essential Schools that use programs designed by Brown University. They employ different methods of teaching and arranging their curriculum. The final decision should be made on the basis of the type of school desired.

Choosing a Catholic School

When considering a Catholic school, parents must remember that there is a strong faith and religious component involved. I point out the religious component, because I realized in the few years that I have helped mentor other parents, especially those who are not Catholic; chose Catholic schools based primarily on proximity, tuition, and discipline. But parents should also be aware that all religious processes are still practiced in these schools; including observing and honoring religious "Holy Days" in accordance with Roman Catholic doctrine.

It is also important that parents check the school's curriculum, student-teacher ratio, academic rigor, teacher qualifications, and extracurricular activities.

Other Factors for Both Types of Schools

When researching schools, parents should attempt to talk to other parents and their students that have attended or who are still attending the school of their choice. Parents should utilize the web or library to look up information on different types of schools and then check with their children to make sure that the schools are a match with their child's interest—the school should be able to provide what both the child and the parents are looking for.

As I said earlier, there are different schools with varying interests and area of concentration. Some schools focus on the arts, some on music or performing arts—most on academics. There are schools that are for gifted students and have a specific curriculum for teaching those students. Parents should also consider the overall size of the school and the size of incoming class.

Parents should check on the number of years the schools, which they are considering, have been in existence. The rule of thumb is that the older a school is, the more alumni there are to speak to and the more established the school. A well-established school may have more endowment funds available and therefore can better help students who are in need of financial aid.

It is equally important for parents to check the school's approach to diversity in terms of faculty and staff, as well as the student body. Many students, especially those from minority populations, feel more comfortable and secure if the school community is racially diverse. Everyone likes to be around people who they can relate to, or who have similar experiences, and who share a cultural heritage. This is valued by many students who like the idea of having someone they can go to when they are having difficulty or experiencing problems accessing the programs in the school.

It should also be noted that accreditation is important for higher education. So parents are encouraged to make sure that the school of their choice is accredited or approved by the state. Another mark to consider is how well a school is regarded by the alumni. More importantly, parents should check to determine if the school's philosophy appeals to them and their child.

The social environment of the school should also be considered. Parents should check to determine if the school is overly competitive or if it is nurturing. This is vital, because that focus impacts how well new students adapt.

Finally, the school's location is very important; in terms of transportation and school attendance. The goal is to choose a school that will disrupt the family the least, but still achieve the set goal.

The overall process can sound very daunting for parents, but carefully choosing the right school is probably one of the most important steps in making sure that the student is content, and parents are not surprised. In other words, parents should make an informed decision that reflects their search and research—ensuring that any school of interest matches what they are looking for and will advance their child's achievement. There should be no guess work or assumptions.

"Parents should make an informed decision that reflects their research. There should be no guess work or assumptions."

---------Author

Chapter 4

Visit the Schools under Consideration

It is beneficial for parents to devote some time to visiting some of the schools that they are considering for enrollment. There are specific considerations to address that will ensure the success of those visits. First, be organized. Have a writing tablet and list each school on a separate page. It is best for parents and their children to have a number of questions and concerns that they need answers to. Be prepared to ask for written explanations and brochures, where applicable, if things are not clear enough.

For boarding schools, it is always a good idea for students to inquire about a sleep-over to actually evaluate and monitor what the environment feels like; this is especially important for co-educational schools. A sleep-over allows parents and their children to closely evaluate both the living conditions and the social behaviors that are evident.

Also when visiting, parents should ask to see different departments; including special programs for children that need them.

If parents are looking for diversity, they should ask for specific numbers regarding racial make-up of students and staff and then verify this during visits to the classrooms as well as the other facilities in the school.

Parents should make sure to arrange a visit with the Dean of Students to get a clear picture of rules and regulations and offenses that may result in suspensions or expulsion. They should also get definite answers for academic questions and rules. It is best to ask for written academic rules so that parents and their children can make time at home to compare the schools, at their convenience. It is important to find out the conditions by which students could be placed on academic probation or even be told to withdraw from school.

Most importantly, parents and their students should speak with student representatives. This will help ensure that they get a current student's version and perspective on school policies and the overall environment. A current Student's Level of Satisfaction Survey is a good guide and measure to judge a school by.

Don't forget to inquire about health services and on-site medical personnel; especially for boarding students. Also, find out about the school's in-patient facility affiliation and insurance protocols.

Application Forms

If the school that is visited meets expectations, an application for enrollment is in order. Most schools, parochial and independent, have a deadline of mid-January for March decisions. Applications that are not received by that time will not be considered.

Just as parents and their students want to know if their choice is a good fit, the chosen school also wants to know exactly who is applying for enrollment—what qualities the child will bring to the school. They also want to know why parents are interested and why they think the school is a good fit for their family.

Consequently, parents should take time to respond to any questionnaires that are distributed by a prospective school. If the parent is not a native English speaker or needs help completing the forms, he or she should seek assistance. In extreme cases, I suggest that parents tell the person that is assisting, what to write; then have them read the responses aloud, and to the best of their ability, make sure that the questionnaire is error-free.

Let the student complete any required essays—on their own. Parents can help by proofreading.

Chapter 5

Financial Aid

Many have argued that America's public schools are, in fact, very good schools and do take care of the majority of children that attend. There is no doubt about the effectiveness of some public schools. Nevertheless, many children may be better served in smaller schools than in larger ones and in classrooms that have more resources than there are in some public schools; this is especially the case in urban areas. Parents know and understand their children and should make a decision based on their child's learning needs.

Although parents may not have abundant financial resources, it is advisable to plan to spend some money toward their child's education. Since education is an investment in the future, parents need to determine how much they can commit toward educating their child; no matter how little.

Parents have to be proactive in this process, because one mistake that many make is to assume that they do not have enough money for an independent and/or parochial school. They should have a positive attitude and find out what financial help is available.

Financial Aid (Catholic Schools)

In Catholic schools, parents who need financial assistance must apply through the school Archdiocese Office. Applicants who are not Catholic may be negatively impacted in the amount given, because the Archdiocese will consider its own parishioners first; before other families. In those cases, non-Catholic families may be required to pay the entire tuition.

Financial Aid (Independent Schools)

Independent schools depend on the charity of donors and fundraising activities to help offset the costs of operating the school, in order to provide some financial aid. Nevertheless, parents should bear in mind that independent schools are generally expensive. Therefore, those who are planning on sending their children to an independent school should start early to save money for that part of their child's education, and be prepared to bear some of the financial burden.

In Independent schools, financial assistance is strictly need-based. So schools have to select students who will benefit from their financial assistance and balance it with those who can pay.

Parents must understand the financial aid process for an independent school. There are a number of forms, which must be completed, but the most important, for this stage of the admission process, are the financial aid forms or the Parents Financial Statement (PFS). The key requirement is documenting income. This is done through the tax forms and W2s. These documents must be received before or on the deadlines established by each school. Parents must be sure to make copies of all tax forms, schedules, and W2s, before sending them to the schools, NAIS' Schools, and Student Services (SSS) by NAIS. Most independent schools generally have April 15th as the deadline for receiving the current year tax forms. This means that parents must file their taxes on time to meet this deadline.

All NAIS applications are governed by the same regulations and deadlines. However, the application for financial aid or Parent's Financial Statement (PFS) is processed separately by NAIS subsidiary (SSS). The application must be submitted on time to SSS by NAIS.

A review of the application forms and all supporting materials are then made by SSS and sent back to individual schools. To make this step easier, I suggest that parents attend financial aid seminars sponsored by Project Step or other education-based social service organizations in their community.

Since Independent schools have to generate money through fundraising, student tuition, and endowment funds, those schools without generous donors may not be able to award a large amount of money to individual students. In addition, aid and awards are given strictly on a first come, first served basis—based on the financial aid forms and the availability of resources at the school. For this reason, parents should plan to contribute toward their children's education—again, no matter how small the amount.

Preparing for Independent schools is a good exercise and a forerunner for college. Parents must make sure that they meet all financial aid deadlines. They should also make sure that they get help in filling out the forms (when necessary) and providing documentation, if needed.

Chapter 6

Final Visits and Interviews

As I stated before, one of the most important processes in preparing for independent or Catholic schools is for both parents and students to visit prospective school campuses. Now, having narrowed down the list, it is crucial to conduct an in-depth visit to the intended school(s). Some students, especially those in the urban areas, need to be familiar with the realities of suburbia private schools and their requirements.

When possible, and where available, students choosing a boarding school should <u>ask</u> to spend at least a night. The sleepover enables the student to get a "feel" for the environment that she or he will eventually go into. As mentioned earlier, this will give the student a glimpse of the boarding policies and help determine if the school will be a fit; or see if she or he can easily adjust to the school's academic and social environment.

Parents, on the other hand, should use this visitation to learn as much as they can about the school—asking questions during interviews with school officials and student escorts. Most schools use senior students and/or class officers as escorts for visiting parents and students. Student escorts provide useful information about what students generally do not like. This type of information and exchange can typically act as a springboard to generate questions during briefing sessions with administrative staff. During the admissions process, parents can also call at any time to get clarification on any questions.

When families are applying to multiple schools, it is best to schedule one interview or visit at a time, to avoid conflict. It is also advisable to start on time and space out the visits to assimilate the differences about the schools and actually compare them.

Parents should set aside time with their children to discuss the positives and negatives of each school. From this discussion, parents will know exactly what they and their children are looking for—they can go through their compilation of schools and see how each school matches up with their expectations and narrow down their school choices and preferences. On the following page is a sample checklist that can be used to rate the school(s) to determine if there is a proper fit. More samples are located in the back of this book.

School Research Checklist

School: _____

Areas	Yes	No
Communicated with other parents		
Communicated with current students		
School curriculum meets needs		
Teacher/student ratio is acceptable		
Age of school is acceptable		
Diversity of school meets expectations		
Accreditation is in place		
Location is reasonable		
Rules and regulations are reasonable		
Student is comfortable with the school		
Financial arrangements are acceptable		
Other:		

Chapter 7

Admission Tests

Both independent and Catholic schools generally expect their students to perform well academically. As a consequence, students must meet certain standards and expectations.

Most independent schools use a standard-based test like the Independent School Entrance Exam (ISEE) for grades 2-12, or another test given by Education Testing Services, (ETS) Princeton. For Catholic Schools, a high school placement test is required, for grades 9-12. It is advisable that students take these tests in advance of submitting an application and other entrance requirements.

In some urban areas, the ISEE is given by the public school district at a certain date; however, the ISEE, as well as the Catholic School Placement Test, can be taken online or at testing centers across the country.

Preparing for admission tests has become quite competitive in recent years. However, all that is required of all students is the same diligence that is required to be successful in school: Students should come to all classes prepared, listen attentively, ask questions when in doubt, do the homework, and practice, practice, practice.

On the night before the test day, parents should encourage students to pack the necessary materials for the next day: pencils, erasers, and a watch. The student should go to bed early so that he or she will be well rested. On the morning of the test, students should have an adequate breakfast, and be on time to avoid panic and anxiety.

The ISEE is given in November of each year by Boston Public Schools and most school districts. Information on the administration of this examination can be obtained by calling Boston Public School's Department of Implementation or visiting the web site at www.bostonpublicschools.org. Parents can also search for independent testing sites on the web. Parents in other locations can contact their local public school department for information.

Other tests required for admissions can be obtained from Educational Testing Services (ETS) in Princeton, New Jersey; prospective schools, or the NAIS and its affiliates in your state or region.

Fortunately, there are centers and organizations that help students prepare for these tests. Currently, Boston Public Schools conduct preparatory classes in the summer. There are other organizations and centers throughout the country that offer preparatory classes for students at different times of the year and charge a nominal fee. It is best for parents to check around to see what works best for their child and serves their purpose; then negotiate appropriately. Parents also have the option of working with a child's current teacher in a specific skill area to get him or her ready for the test.

"Parents should set aside time with their children to discuss the positives and negatives of each school."

---------Author

Chapter 8

Acceptance

Being accepted into an independent or parochial school creates a wonderful feeling for the student. Some get accepted to multiple schools; depending on the number applied to. Once an offer is made, parents should read through all documents and requirements. I always highlight important points for later reference. I encourage parents to either do this or use any technique that will work for them.

Despite the fact that parents and their children have done the initial screening by visiting schools and submitting applications, this is the last opportunity that they will have to closely scrutinize the schools and choose the one that will be the best fit.

The letter of offer is usually very detailed. I advise parents to be sure that they understand exactly what is intended before signing the contract. If the wording is ambiguous or confusing, call the school or get someone else to explain it. This is particularly important with the financial aid packet and the payment schedules. Parents must also be sure to check with the bookstore regarding their purchase agreement as well as acceptable payment methods for books and school supplies.

Most offers are accompanied by a return letter for the purpose of either acceptance or rejection of the offer. There is also a requirement for a deposit, with a stated deadline. This is the school's way of making sure that the slot will be retained or given up to be offered to another student.

Another purpose that the acceptance offer serves is for parents to be sure that the level of financial involvement stated in the offer is at the level that they can comfortably afford. It is the final time for parents to review their financial options to make sure that an independent or parochial education is appropriate for their family. For those parents in the Boston area, it could be a time to consider other alternatives like the three Examination Schools, Boston Latin, Latin Academy, or O'Bryant; if, that is, their student receives placement offers. For those in other cities around the country, it could be a good time to also consider charter schools, magnet schools, or other alternative schools.

Chapter 9

Other Considerations

Transportation

Most parents that are interested in transferring their student into an independent school are usually those living in urban areas; with large and crowded public schools. In Massachusetts however, almost all of the independent schools are located in the suburbs. That means that parents will have to arrange transportation for their children or plan on driving them to the school. When applicable, parents need to provide information to the school, in writing, about their child's pickup time. For most schools that provide their own transportation, a fee is usually attached.

Vacations

It is important that parents start early to plan for their child's vacation times. This is important due to the fact that independent schools have different school year calendars and class schedules compared to public schools.

Custodianship and Visitations

In the United States, the statistics on divorce are well documented. According to the US census bureau, 50% of all marriages end in divorce; and the divorce rate on second and subsequent marriages is even higher. For this reason, it is important for divorced parents to state, in writing, custody arrangements as well as pickups and visitation arrangements for boarding students. If there are any changes, parents must make sure to get the information to school authorities in a timely manner.

Health Care Services

Independent schools are responsible for caring for the wellbeing of their students and do provide simple health care services. Any student that requires urgent medical attention is sent to a hospital, which has been designated by the school, to provide the needed care. In those cases parents are responsible for the bill. Therefore, parents should indicate if they have family health insurance as well as dental insurance. If a child is not covered in a family health insurance plan, the school may charge for health insurance coverage. As in all schools, immunizations are mandatory—current records must be maintained. A physical examination is also mandatory for student athletes.

Participation

The most important way for a student to have a happy and successful independent or parochial school experience is to follow the rules of the school. For parents, being involved in the school community is also very important; especially as a way to show support for their own children.

Donations and fund raising are always welcomed by the schools, since those are some of the ways that they can generate funds to support the school and its students.

Call the respective schools and ask questions if there are problems or if you, as the parent, have any concerns.

I sincerely hope that you and your child have a successful independent or parochial school experience.

School Research Checklist

School: _____

Areas	Yes	No
Communicated with other parents		
Communicated with current students		
School curriculum meets needs		
Teacher/student ratio is acceptable		
Age of school is acceptable		
Diversity of school meets expectations		
Accreditation is in place		
Location is reasonable		
Rules and regulations are reasonable		
Student is comfortable with the school		
Financial arrangements are acceptable		
Other:		

School Research Checklist

School: _____

Areas	Yes	No
Communicated with other parents		
Communicated with current students		
School curriculum meets needs		
Teacher/student ratio is acceptable		
Age of school is acceptable		
Diversity of school meets expectations		
Accreditation is in place		
Location is reasonable		
Rules and regulations are reasonable		
Student is comfortable with the school		
Financial arrangements are acceptable		
Other:		

School Research Checklist

School: _____

Areas	Yes	No
Communicated with other parents		
Communicated with current students		
School curriculum meets needs		
Teacher/student ratio is acceptable		
Age of school is acceptable		
Diversity of school meets expectations		
Accreditation is in place		
Location is reasonable		
Rules and regulations are reasonable		
Student is comfortable with the school		
Financial arrangements are acceptable		
Other:		

School Research Checklist

School: _____

Areas	Yes	No
Communicated with other parents		
Communicated with current students		
School curriculum meets needs		
Teacher/student ratio is acceptable		
Age of school is acceptable		
Diversity of school meets expectations		
Accreditation is in place		
Location is reasonable		
Rules and regulations are reasonable		
Student is comfortable with the school		
Financial arrangements are acceptable		
Other:		

Also from Anointed Life Publishing

DISCOVERING YOUR ANOINTING NUMBERS
By Carolyn Chambers

In her life-changing new book, Carolyn Chambers helps readers discover their anointing numbers and empowers them to fight life's great battle-themselves. Simply put—everyone is at war with themselves. But, walking anointed is something everyone can achieve. In, *"Discovering Your Anointing Numbers: Allow me to introduce You to Yourself,"* Carolyn Chambers examines the influence that birth demographics have on human behavior. This is a compelling read for all.

THE ANOINTED LIFE – CRUCIFYING THE FLESH
By Carolyn Chambers

Thoughts received from the flesh alienate us from the grace of God; while those received from the spirit bring righteousness, peace, and joy. The flesh cunningly attacks the will, the mind, and the emotions; keeping us in a state of immaturity and alienated from our inheritance through fear, doubt, and unbelief. However, thoughts received from the spirit position us to live the anointed life—a life lived under the influence of the Holy Spirit.

We invite you to visit our website at:
Anointed Life Publishing

www.anointedlifepublishing.com

www.ingramcontent.com/pod-product-compliance
Lightning Source LLC
Chambersburg PA
CBHW072112290426
44110CB00014B/1893